THEY BUILT ME FOR **FREEDOM**

THEY BUILT ME FREED

THE STORY OF JUNETEENTH AND HOUSTON'S EMANCIPATION PARK

For the Duncan and Ellis families, generations to come
and generations who've gone before. —T.D.E.

For Aunt Jeannette, who fought for a just world
in the court and at home. —J.M.

Balzer + Bray is an imprint of HarperCollins Publishers.
They Built Me for Freedom: The Story of Juneteenth and Houston's Emancipation Park • Text copyright © 2024
by Tonya Duncan Ellis • Illustrations copyright © 2024 by Jenin Mohammed • All riaghts reserved. Manufactured in
Italy. • No part of this book may be used or reproduced in any manner whatsoever without written permission except
in the case of brief quotations embodied in critical articles and reviews. For information address HarperCollins
Children's Books, a division of HarperCollins Publishers, 195 Broadway, New York, NY 10007.
www.harpercollinschildrens.com
Library of Congress Control Number: 2023943338 • ISBN 978-0-06-328605-4 • Typography by Chelsea C. Donaldson
24 25 26 27 28 RTLO 10 9 8 7 6 5 4 3 2 1 • First Edition

FOR
OM

Written by

TONYA DUNCAN ELLIS

Illustrated by

JENIN MOHAMMED

BALZER + BRAY
An Imprint of HarperCollins Publishers

When people visit me, they are free . . .

EMANCIPATION PARK

ACQUIRED 1918

. . . to run,

play,

gather,

and rejoice.

They built me to **remember**.

June 19, 1865.
The day enslaved people found out the truth.
They could work for their own money.
Start their own families.
Live their own lives.

No more beatings.
No more chains.
No more being sent away from loved ones.
Finally, they were free.

They built me to show they were **strong**.

Gathering together.
Raising money.
Buying ten acres of land.
Giving me life.

They built me to **celebrate**.
Stately horses prance with proud cowboys on their backs.
A gospel choir croons "Lift Every Voice and Sing."

Families feast from picnic baskets bursting with barbecue.
Their dancing feet make my grasses sway.

They built me to **play**.
Beating the heat in the big pool.

Munching cottony treats.
Hearing music float through the Third Ward.
Watching baseballs rocket toward the clouds.

They built me to **give thanks**.
For the power to praise.

For a place to raise hands in peace.
For my benches, where they rest and breathe
in the busy, city, streets.

They built me to **fight**.
Challenging those who discriminated
against them because they were Black.

Marching for justice.
Demanding equal rights.

As the years passed, some forgot.
Skyscrapers replaced the trees that once hugged my fields.

Trash scurried across the ground.
Broken chains sagged from swing sets.

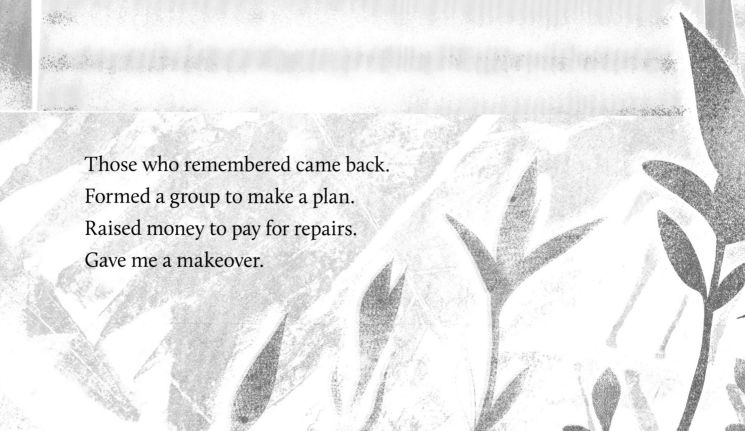

Those who remembered came back.
Formed a group to make a plan.
Raised money to pay for repairs.
Gave me a makeover.

It was a new day.

Now a different generation visits.
Scampering on splash pads.

Cheering at Miss Juneteenth
pageants and parades.

Smiling as skaters rock, roll, and bounce.
Admiring the art that adorns me like jewelry.

While they enjoy my beautiful grounds,
they recall their ancestors and all they overcame.
Standing strong.
Walking proud.
Singing songs of jubilee . . . running free.

They built me for **freedom**.

The oldest public green space in Texas, Emancipation Park is an important symbol of American freedom.

In 1863, President Abraham Lincoln signed the Emancipation Proclamation, ending slavery in the Confederacy—the southern half of the country that seceded from the United States, beginning the Civil War. But the news spread slowly through the Confederate states and territories, and the 250,000 enslaved people in Texas didn't find out they were free until two years later, on June 19, 1865, the day Union general Gordon Granger rode into Galveston, Texas, along with his troops. The date came to be known as Freedom Day, then, later, Juneteenth.

To commemorate the event, the Reverends Jack Yates and Elias Dibble, Richard Allen, and Richard Brock, all church and community leaders in Houston, raised nearly one thousand dollars to buy ten acres of land in an area in the southwest of the city called the Third Ward, naming the land Emancipation Park. During the time of Jim Crow laws and racial segregation, Emancipation Park would be the only public park and public swimming pool facility in Houston open to African Americans. The land for Emancipation Park was purchased in 1872; it was later officially donated to the city of Houston, which established it as a municipal park in 1918. In time it became a vibrant, year-round center of community activity.

After the civil rights movement and integration, wealthier African Americans moved from the predominately Black Third Ward area, and Emancipation Park fell into disrepair. For over thirty years, the park languished and eventually stopped hosting Juneteenth celebrations. This prompted Third Ward residents to raise money to revitalize the space. Philip Freelon, the architect who designed the National Museum of African American History and Culture in Washington, DC, was brought on to design the renovation plans. The work was completed, and Emancipation Park was rededicated in 2017.

In the years after Emancipation Park was built, Juneteenth celebrations spread throughout Texas and, eventually, the nation. Texas was the first state, in 1980, to make Juneteenth a holiday. In 2021, President Joe Biden signed the Juneteenth National Independence Day Act into law, making Juneteenth a federal holiday as well.